❄ WE KNIT YOU A ❄
MERRY CHRISTMAS

First published in the United Kingdom
in 2012 by
Collins & Brown
10 Southcombe Street
London
W14 0RA

An imprint of Anova Books Company Ltd

Distributed in the United States and Canada by
Sterling Publishing Co, 387 Park Avenue South,
New York, NY 10016-8810, USA

ISBN 978-1-90844-921-4

A CIP catalogue for this book is available from the
British Library.

10 9 8 7 6 5 4 3 2 1

Reproduction by Mission Productions Ltd, Hong Kong
Printed and bound by Toppan Leefung Printing Ltd, China

This book can be ordered direct from the publisher at
www.anovabooks.com

❄ WE KNIT YOU A ❄ MERRY CHRISTMAS

DEBBIE HARROLD

COLLINS & BROWN

CONTENTS

BRUSSELS SPROUT

Materials
* Yarn such as:
  Patons Fab DK, approx. 68m/25g
  ball (100% acrylic)
  1 ball in Light green 2317
  1 ball in White 2306
* One pair of 3.75mm needles
* Tapestry needle
* Toy filling
* One pair of 10mm wiggle eyes
* PVA glue or a glue gun

Tension
22 stitches and 30 rows over 10cm
stocking stitch.

Body and head
Using 3.75mm needles and light green
yarn, cast on 6 sts.
Row 1 (WS): Purl.
Row 2: [Inc 1] 6 times. (12 sts)
Row 3: [Inc 1, p1] 6 times. (18 sts)
Work 10 rows in stocking stitch.
Row 14: [K1, k2tog] 6 times. (12 sts)
Row 15: [P2tog] 6 times. (6 sts)
Row 16: [K2tog] 3 times. (3 sts)
Break off yarn and thread through
stitches on needle.
Draw tight and secure the end.

Leaves (make 6)
Using 3.75mm needles, light green yarn
and leaving a 10cm tail, cast on 3 sts.
Row 1 (WS): Purl.
Row 2: [Inc 1] twice, k1. (5 sts)
Row 3: Purl.
Row 4: Inc 1, knit to the last 2 sts, inc 1,
k1. (7 sts)
Row 5: Purl.
Repeat last 2 rows once more. (9 sts)
Row 8: K2togtbl, knit to the last 2 sts,
k2tog. (7 sts)
Row 9: Purl.
Repeat last 2 rows twice more. (3 sts)
Cast off.

Making up
For the body and head, partially sew
up the side seam using mattress stitch
or backstitch, insert stuffing and
complete the seam.
Using the cast-on tail, attach three leaves
evenly around the base of the body.
Then attach the remaining three leaves
evenly around the base of the body,
overlapping the first three leaves.
Using picture as guide, glue eyes to the
head section.
For the beard and moustache, cut
shapes out of felt and glue in place just
underneath the eyes.
For the hat, use the hat pattern from
Ha Pea Christmas (page 8) or Ho, Ho,
Ho (page 26) or make a hat from felt.

CHILL OUT

Materials

* Yarn such as:
  Patons Fab DK, approx. 68m/25g
  ball (100% acrylic)
  1 ball in Red 2323
  1 ball in Green 2319
* One pair of 3.75mm needles
* Tapestry needle
* Toy filling
* Short length of white yarn
* One pair of 5mm wiggle eyes
* PVA glue or a glue gun
* Short length of fine craft wire
* One red craft pipe cleaner
* Pencil
* Wire cutters
* Small piece of yellow paper

Tension

22 stitches and 30 rows over 10cm
stocking stitch.

Body and head

Using 3.75mm needles and red yarn,
cast on 3 sts.
Row 1 (RS): Knit.
Row 2: Purl.
Row 3: [Inc 1] twice, k1. (5 sts)
Work 3 rows in stocking stitch.
Row 7: Inc 1, knit to the last 2 sts, inc 1,
k1. (7 sts)
Work 3 rows in stocking stitch.
Repeat the last 4 rows 5 times more.
(17 sts)
Row 31: [K3, k2tog] 3 times, k2. (14 sts)
Row 32: Purl.

Row 33: [K2, k2tog] 3 times, k2. (11 sts)
Row 34: Purl.
Break off red yarn and join in green.

Stalk

Row 35: [K2tog, k1] 3 times, k2tog. (7 sts)
Row 36: Purl.
Row 37: [K2tog, k1] twice, k1. (5 sts)
Row 38: P2tog, p1, p2tog. (3 sts)
Work a further 6 rows in garter stitch.
Break off yarn and thread through
stitches on needle.
Draw tight and secure the end.

Making up

For the body and head, partially sew
up the side seam, using mattress stitch
or backstitch, insert stuffing and
complete the seam.
Using the pipe cleaner, make two arms
with hands; then attach them to the
body of the chilli.
Using picture as guide, embroider a
mouth with the white yarn and, using
glue, attach eyes to the head section.
For the spectacles, wrap the craft wire
around a pencil and trim the ends.
Use the yellow paper to make a crown
to fit the top of the chilli.

HA PEA CHRISTMAS

Materials

* Yarn such as:
  Patons Fab DK, approx. 68m/25g ball (100% acrylic)
  1 ball in Green 2317
  1 ball in White 2306
  1 ball in Red 2323
* One pair of 3.75mm needles
* Tapestry needle
* Toy filling
* One pair of 10mm wiggle eyes
* PVA glue or a glue gun
* One red craft pipe cleaner
* A set of sticks and skis for a small toy

Tension

22 stitches and 26 rows over 10cm stocking stitch.

Body and head

Using 3.75mm needles and green yarn, cast on 6 sts.
Row 1 (RS): [Inc 1, knitwise] 6 times. (12 sts)
Row 2: Purl.
Row 3: [Inc 1, k1] 6 times. (18 sts)
Row 4: Purl.
Row 5: [Inc 1, k2] 6 times. (24 sts)
Work 9 rows in stocking stitch.
Row 15: K1 [k2tog, k2] 5 times, k2tog, k1. (18 sts)
Row 16: Purl.
Row 17: [K2tog, k1] 6 times. (12 sts)
Row 18: Purl.

Row 19: [K2tog] 6 times. (6 sts)
Break off yarn and thread through stitches on needle.
Draw tight and secure the end.

Legs (make 2)

Using 3.75mm needles and green yarn, cast on 5 sts.
Work 12 rows in stocking stitch.
Break off yarn and thread through stitches on needle.
Draw tight and secure the end.

Arms (make 2)

Using 3.75mm needles and green yarn, cast on 5 sts.
Work 10 rows in stocking stitch.
Break off yarn and thread through stitches on needle.
Draw tight and secure the end.

Hat

Using 3.75mm needles and white yarn, cast on 20 sts.
Work 4 rows in garter stitch.
Break off white yarn and join in red.
Row 5: Purl.
Row 6: K1, k2togtbl, knit to the last 3 sts, k2tog, k1. (18 sts)
Repeat the last 2 rows until 6 sts remain.
Row 19: Purl.
Break off yarn and thread through stitches on needle.
Draw tight and secure the end.

Bobble

Using 3.75mm needles and white yarn, cast on 5 sts.
Work 3 rows in garter stitch.
Break off yarn and thread through stitches on needle.
Draw tight and secure the end.

Making up

For the body and head, partially sew up side seam, using mattress stitch or backstitch, insert stuffing and complete the seam.
For the hands and arms, wrap a length of red pipe cleaner around the top of the ski stick then wrap the arms around the pipe cleaner, cut the pipe cleaner to length and using matching yarn sew up the side seam.
Wrap the legs around a matching length of pipe cleaner and sew up the side seam. Bend one end of each leg to create a foot.
Attach the legs and arms to the body and head.
Using picture as guide and red yarn embroider the mouth using straight stitches and glue the eyes to the head.
Using matching yarn, sew up the side seam of the hat and attach the bobble.
Attach the hat, skis and sticks to the pea.

TURKEY

Materials

* Yarn such as:
  Sirdar Classics DK Bonus, approx.
  280m/100g ball (100% acrylic)
  1 ball in Brown 947
  Patons Fab DK, approx. 68m/25g
  ball (100% acrylic)
  1 ball in Yellow 2302
  1 ball in Beige 2331
  1 ball in Cream 2307
* One pair of 3.75mm needles
* Tapestry needle
* Toy filling
* One pair of 10mm wiggle eyes
* Small piece of red felt
* PVA glue or a glue gun

Tension

22 stitches and 30 rows over 10cm
stocking stitch.

Body

Using 3.75mm needles and brown yarn,
cast on 6 sts. Work in garter stitch.
Row 1 (WS): Purl.
Row 2: [Inc 1 knitwise] 6 times. (12 sts)
Row 3: Knit.
Row 4: [Inc 1, k1] 6 times. (18 sts)
Row 5: Knit.
Row 6: [Inc 1, k2] 6 times. (24 sts)
Row 7: Knit.
Row 8: [Inc 1, k3] 6 times. (30 sts)
Work 13 rows in garter stitch.
Row 22: [K3, k2tog] 6 times. (24 sts)
Row 23: Knit.
Row 24: [K2, k2tog] 6 times. (18 sts)
Row 25: Knit.
Row 26: [K1, k2tog] 6 times. (12 sts)
Row 27: Knit.
Row 28: [K2tog] 6 times. (6 sts)
Row 29: Knit.
Break off yarn and thread through
stitches on needle.
Draw tight and secure the end.

Beak and head

Using 3.75mm needles and yellow yarn,
cast on 4 sts. Work in garter stitch.
Row 1 (WS): Purl.
Row 2: [Inc 1 knitwise] 4 times. (8 sts)
Work 5 rows in garter stitch.
Row 8: [Inc 1] 8 times. (16 sts)
Break off yellow yarn and join in
brown.
Row 9: Knit.
Row 10: [Inc 1, k3] 4 times. (20 sts)
Row 11: Knit.

Row 12: [Inc 1, k4] 4 times. (24 sts)
Work 9 rows in garter stitch.
Row 22: [K2tog] 12 times. (12 sts)
Row 23: Knit.
Row 24: [K2tog] 6 times. (6 sts)
Row 25: Knit.
Break off yarn and thread through
stitches on needle.
Draw tight and secure the end.

Tail

Using 3.75mm needles and brown
yarn, cast on 15 sts.
Row 1 (RS): [K1, p1] 7 times, k1.
Row 2: [P1, k1] 7 times, p1.
Row 3: [K1, inc 1 purlwise] 7 times, k1.
(22 sts)
Row 4: [P1, k2] 7 times, p1.
Row 5: [K1, p2] 7 times, k1.
Row 6: Repeat row 4.
Row 7: [K1, inc 1 purlwise, p1] 7 times,
k1. (29 sts)
Row 8: [P1, k3] 7 times, p1.
Break off brown yarn and join in beige.
Row 9: [K1, p3] 7 times, k1.
Row 10: Repeat row 8.
Row 11: [K1, inc 1 purlwise, p2] 7 times,
k1. (36 sts)
Row 12: [P1, k4] 7 times, p1.
Row 13: [K1, p4] 7 times, k1.
Row 14: Repeat row 12.
Break off beige yarn and join in cream.
Row 15: [K1, inc 1 purlwise, p3] 7 times,
k1. (43 sts)
Row 16: [P1, k5] 7 times, p1.
Row 17: [K1, p5] 7 times, k1.

Repeat the last 2 rows once more.

Row 20: Repeat row 16.

Row 21: [K1, p2tog, p3] 7 times, k1. (36 sts)

Break off cream yarn and join in beige.

Repeat rows 12–14 once more.

Row 25: [K1, p2tog, p2] 7 times, k1. (29 sts)

Row 26: [P1, k3] 7 times, p1.

Row 27: [K1, p3] 7 times, k1.

Break off beige yarn and join in brown.

Row 28: Repeat row 26.

Row 29: [K1, p2tog, p1] 7 times, k1. (22 sts)

Repeat rows 4–6 once more.

Row 33: [K1, p2tog] 7 times, k1. (15 sts)

Repeat rows 1–2 once more.

Cast of in rib pattern set.

Making up

For the body, head and tail pieces, partially sew up side seams, using mattress stitch or backstitch, insert stuffing and complete the seam.

Using matching yarn, work a line of running stitches around the base of the beak and gather slightly, using glue, attach the eyes.

Using matching yarn attach the head and tail pieces to the body.

For the turkey's wattle, draw a long thin rectangle with an oval shape at each short side about 8cm long and 1cm deep at the widest point onto red felt, cut out and glue in place.

For the hat, use the hat pattern from Ha Pea Christmas (page 8) or Ho, Ho, Ho (page 26) or make a hat from felt.

GO CRACKERS!

Materials

To make one cracker:

* Yarn such as:
  Patons Fab DK, approx. 68m/25g
  ball (100% acrylic)
  1 ball in Green 2319 or Red 2323
  (MC)
  1 ball in Red 2323 or White 2306
  (CC)
* One pair of 3.75mm needles
* Tapestry needle
* Toy filling
* One inner cardboard roll from
  kitchen towel
* One pair of 5mm wiggle eyes
* Small pieces of white and red felt
* PVA glue or a glue gun
* One green or white craft pipe
  cleaner
* Short length of red or white 5mm,
  organza ribbon

Tension

22 stitches and 30 rows over 10cm
stocking stitch.

Body and head (make 1)

Using 3.75mm needles and MC yarn,
cast on 25 sts.
*Row 1(RS): Knit.
Row 2: Purl.
Break off MC yarn and join in CC.
Work 2 rows in stocking stitch.
Break off CC yarn and join in MC.
Repeat from * once more.
Work 46 rows in stocking stitch.
**Break off MC yarn and join in CC.
Work 2 rows in stocking stitch.
Break off CC yarn and join in MC.
Work 2 rows in stocking stitch.
Repeat from ** once more.
Cast off.

Making up

For the body and head, partially sew
up the side seam, using mattress stitch
or backstitch.
Insert a 10cm length of kitchen towel
inner cardboard roll lightly stuffed with
toy filling. Secure the ends with
lengths of ribbon tied into a bow.
Using picture as guide and using glue,
attach eyes and felt mouth and teeth
to the head sections.
Using the pipe cleaners, make two
arms with hands; then attach them to
the body of each cracker.
For the hat, use the hat pattern from
Ha Pea Christmas (page 8) or Ho, Ho,
Ho (page 26) or make a hat from felt.

LET IT SNOW

Materials

To make one snowball:

* Yarn such as:
  Patons Fab DK, approx. 68m/25g
  ball (100% acrylic)
  1 ball in White 2306
* One pair of 3.75mm needles
* Tapestry needle
* Toy filling
* Short lengths of black and red yarn
* One pair of 5mm wiggle eyes
* Small pieces of coloured tissue
  paper.

Tension

22 stitches and 26 rows over 10cm
stocking stitch.

Body and head (make 1)

Using 3.75mm needles and white yarn,
cast on 5 sts.
Row 1 (RS): [Inc 1 knitwise] 5 times.
(10 sts)
Row 2: [Inc 1 knitwise] 10 times.
(20 sts)
Row 3: [Inc 1, k1] 10 times. (30 sts)
Starting with a knit row, work 16 rows
in stocking stitch.
Row 20: [K2tog, k1] 10 times. (20 sts)
Row 21: [K2tog] 10 times. (10 sts)
Row 22: [K2tog] 5 times. (5 sts)
Break off yarn and thread through
stitches on needle.
Draw tight and secure the end.

Making up

For the body and head, with the
reverse stocking stitch side facing
outwards, partially sew up side seam,
using mattress stitch or backstitch,
insert stuffing and complete the seam.
Using picture as guide and red or black
yarn, embroider the mouths using
backstitch, using glue, attach the eyes.
Use the coloured tissue paper to make
a crown to fit the top of the snowball.

GINGERBREAD

Materials

* Yarn such as:
  Sirdar Classics DK Bonus, approx.
  280m/100g ball (100% acrylic)
  1 ball in Copper 843
* One pair of 3.75mm needles
* Stitch holder
* Tapestry needle
* Toy filling
* Short lengths of white and
  red yarn

Tension

22 stitches and 30 rows over 10cm
stocking stitch.

GINGERBREAD MALE
Body and head (make 2)
Right leg piece

Using 3.75mm needles and copper
yarn, cast on 4 sts.
Row 1 (WS): Purl.
Row 2: Inc 1, knit to last 2 sts, inc 1, k1.
(6 sts)
Row 3: Purl.
Row 4: K1, k2togtbl, k1, inc 1, k1. (6 sts)
Row 5: Purl.
Repeat last 2 rows 5 times more.
Break off yarn and transfer stitches
onto a stitch holder.

Left leg piece

Using 3.75mm needles and copper
yarn, cast on 4 sts.
Row 1 (WS): Purl.
Row 2: Inc 1, knit to last 2 sts, inc 1, k1.
(6 sts)
Row 3: Purl.
Row 4: Inc 1, k2, k2tog, k1. (6 sts)
Row 5: Purl.
Repeat last 2 rows 5 times more.
Break off yarn.

Body

Join the legs by working across the
stitches of both legs as follows:
with the stitches for the left leg still
on the needle and the needle tip to
the right, transfer the stitches for the
right leg from the stitch holder, right
side facing, onto the same needle. Join
in yarn.
Row 16: K5, k2tog (last st from Right
leg piece and first st of Left leg piece),

cont to work across the Left leg piece
stitches, k5. (11 sts)
**Work 9 rows in stocking stitch,
ending with a purl row.

Arms

Row 26: Cast on 8 sts, knit to end. (19 sts)
Row 27: Cast on 8 sts, purl to end.
(27 sts)
Work 2 rows in stocking stitch.
Row 30: Cast off 8 sts, knit to end. (19 sts)
Row 31: Cast off 8 sts, purl to end. (11 sts)
Row 32: K1, k2togtbl, knit to last 3 sts,
k2tog, k1. (9 sts)
Row 33: P1, P2tog, purl to last 3 sts,
p2togtbl, p1. (7 sts)
Row 34: Knit.

Head

Row 35: Inc 1, purl to last 2 sts, inc 1, k1.
(9 sts)
Row 36: Inc 1, knit to last 2 sts, inc 1, k1.
(11 sts)
Work 3 rows in stocking stitch.
Row 40: K1, k2tog, knit to last 3 sts,
k2tog, k1. (9 sts)
Row 41: Purl.
Repeat last 2 rows 3 times more. (3 sts)
Cast off.

GINGERBREAD FEMALE
Body and head (make 2)
Skirt
Using 3.75mm needles and copper yarn, cast on 35 sts.

Row 1 (WS): Purl.

Row 2: K4, [sl1, k2tog, psso, k3] 5 times, k1. (25 sts)

Row 3: Purl.

Row 4: K3, [sl1, k2tog, psso, k1] 5 times, k2. (15 sts)

Work 3 rows in stocking stitch.

Row 8: K1, k2togtbl, knit to last 3 sts, k2tog, k1. (13 sts)

Row 9: Purl.

Row 10: K1, k2togtbl, knit to last 3 sts, k2tog, k1. (11 sts)

Continue from ** on Gingerbread Male Body and Head.

Making up
Make up Gingerbread Male and Gingerbread Female as follows: for the body and head, partially sew the two pieces together using mattress stitch or backstitch, insert stuffing and complete the seam. Using picture as guide, embroider the mouth using chain stitch, the eyes and buttons using satin stitch.

CHOIR BOYS

Materials

To make one choir boy:

⁜ Yarn such as:
Patons Fab DK, approx. 68m/25g
ball (100% acrylic)
1 ball in Red (R) 2323
1 ball in White (W) 2306
1 ball in Skin 2328
1 ball in Brown 2309
Sirdar Funky Fur approx. 90m/50g
ball (100% polyester)
1 ball in Black 510
⁜ One pair of 3.75mm needles
⁜ Tapestry needle
⁜ One inner cardboard roll from rolls
of toilet tissue
⁜ One pair of 10mm wiggle eyes
⁜ Short lengths of both pink and
gold embroidery thread
⁜ Small amount of thin card

Tension

22 stitches and 30 rows over 10cm
stocking stitch.

Body and head (make 1)

Using 3.75mm needles and red yarn,
cast on 32 sts.
Work 2 rows in garter stitch.
Starting with a knit row, work 4 rows
in stocking stitch.
Row 7: K1, k2togtbl, knit to the last
3 sts, k2tog, k1. (30 sts)
Work 3 rows in stocking stitch.
Repeat the last 4 rows once more.
(28 sts)

Break off red yarn, join in white.
Repeat the last 4 rows 3 times more.
(22 sts)
Row 27: K1, k2togtbl, k5, join in red
yarn, [k1R, k1W] twice, k1R, k6W,
k2togW, k1W. (20 sts)
Using the intarsia method work the
following rows.
Row 28: P7W, p6R, p7W.
Row 29: K7W, k6R, k7W.
Row 30: P7W, p6R, p7W.
Row 31: K1W, k2togtblW, k4W, k6R,
k4W, k2togW, k1W. (18 sts)
Row 32: P6W, p6R, p6W.
Row 33: K6W, k6R, k6W.
Row 34: P6W, p6R, p6W.
Row 35: K1W, k2togtblW, k3W, k6R,
k3W, k2togW, k1W. (16 sts)
Break off red and white yarn, join
in skin.
Row 36: [P2tog] 8 times. (8 sts)
Row 37: [K2tog] 4 times. (4 sts)
Row 38: [Inc 1 purlwise] 4 times. (8 sts)
Row 39: [Inc 1 knitwise] 8 times.
(16 sts)
Row 40: [Inc 1, p1] 8 times. (24 sts)
Work 14 rows of stocking stitch.
Row 55: [K2tog] 12 times. (12 sts)
Row 56: [P2tog] 6 times. (6 sts)
Break off yarn and thread through
stitches on needle.
Draw tight and secure the end.

Arms (make 2)

Using 3.75mm needles and white yarn,
cast on 10 sts.

Starting with a knit row, work 8 rows
in stocking stitch.
Break off white yarn, join in red.
Work 8 rows in stocking stitch.
Break off red yarn, join in skin.
Work 5 rows in stocking stitch.
Row 22: [P2tog] 5 times. (5 sts)
Break off yarn and thread through
stitches on needle.
Draw tight and secure the end.

Bottom frill (make 1)

Using 3.75mm needles and white yarn,
cast on 28 sts.
Starting with a knit row, work 2 rows in
stocking stitch.
Row 3: [Yfwd, k2tog] 14 times.
Work 2 rows in stocking stitch.
Cast off.

Neck frill (make 1)

Using 3.75mm needles and white yarn,
cast on 10 sts.
Knit 1 row.
Cast off.

Base

Using 3.75mm needles and red yarn,
cast on 8 sts.
Row 1 (WS) (and every WS row): Purl.
Row 2: [Inc 1] 8 times. (16 sts)
Row 4: [Inc 1, k1] 8 times. (24 sts)
Row 6: K1, [inc 1, k2] 7 times, inc 1, k1.
(32 sts)
Row 7: Purl.
Cast off.

Hymn book

Using 3.75mm needles and brown
yarn, cast on 8 sts.
Work 12 rows in stocking stitch.
Cast off.

Making up

For the body and head, sew up side
seam, using mattress stitch or
backstitch. Insert an inner cardboard
roll from a roll of toilet tissue and
insert stuffing. For the base, sew up
the side seam and stitch to the bottom
of the body.

Using picture as guide, for the hair,
working from crown outwards, coil
and stitch in place the fur yarn to the
top of the head; embroider the mouth
using backstitch; glue eyes to the
head section.

Attach the arms to the body and head,
then wrap the neck frill around the
neck and stitch the shorter edges
together and finally, wrap the bottom
frill around the lower edge of the
white surplice, and stitch in place.
For the hymn books, with reverse
stocking stitch facing outwards, fold
the knitted fabric in half lengthways,
cut card to match, wrap the fabric
around the card and stitch the edges
together. Fold in half and wrap gold
thread around the spine.

SNAPPY CHRISTMAS

Materials

* ❋ Yarn such as:
  Sirdar Country Style DK, approx.
  155m/50g ball (40% nylon, 30%wool,
  30% acrylic)
  1 ball in Light Brown 477
  Sirdar Classics DK Bonus, approx.
  280m/100g ball (100% acrylic)
  1 ball in Green 904
  Patons Fab DK, approx. 68m/25g
  ball (100% acrylic)
  1 ball in Pink 2304
* ❋ One pair of 3.75mm needles
* ❋ Tapestry needle
* ❋ Toy filling
* ❋ One pair of 5mm wiggle eyes
* ❋ PVA glue or a glue gun
* ❋ Small piece of white felt
* ❋ Sewing needle and matching
  thread

Tension

22 stitches and 26 rows over 10cm
stocking stitch.

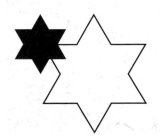

Underbody – tail to head

Using 3.75mm needles and light brown
yarn, cast on 3 sts.
Row 1 (WS): Purl.
Row 2: [Inc 1] twice, k1. (5 sts)
Row 3: Inc 1, purl to last 2 sts, inc 1, p1.
(7 sts)
Row 4: Inc 1, knit to last 2 sts, inc 1, k1.
(9 sts)
Repeat the last 2 rows once more.
(13 sts)
Row 7: Purl.
Row 8: Inc 1, knit to last 2 sts, inc 1, k1.
(15 sts)
Repeat the last 2 rows 5 times more.
(25 sts)
Row 19: Purl.
Row 20: K1, k2togtbl, knit to last 3 sts,
k2tog, k1. (23 sts)
Row 21: P1, p2tog, purl to last 3 sts,
p2togtbl, k1. (21 sts)
Repeat the last 2 rows 3 times more.
(9 sts)
Work 4 rows in stocking stitch.
Row 32: K1, k2togtbl, knit to last 3 sts,
k2tog, k1. (7 sts)
Work 9 rows in stocking stitch.
Row 42: K1, k2togtbl, knit to last 3 sts,
k2tog, k1. (5 sts)
Cast off.

Top body – tail to head

Using 3.75mm needles and green yarn,
cast on 3 sts.

Work as for Underbody but work in
moss stitch throughout:
RS: (K1, p1) rep to end.
WS: (K1, p1) to end.

Legs (make 4)

Using 3.75mm needles and green yarn,
cast on 10 sts.
Starting with a knit row, work 4 rows
in stocking stitch.
Row 5: K1, k2togtbl, knit to the last
2 sts, inc 1, k1.
Row 6: Purl.
Repeat the last 2 rows 3 times more.
Row 13: [K2tog] 5 times. (5 sts)
Break off yarn and thread through
stitches on needle.
Draw tight and secure the end.

Mouth

Using 3.75mm needles and pink yarn,
cast on 4 sts.
Row 1 (WS): Purl.
Row 2: Inc 1, knit to last 2 sts, inc 1, k1.
(6 sts)
Row 3: Inc 1, purl to last 2 sts, inc 1, k1.
(8 sts)
Work 12 rows in stocking stitch.
Row 16: Inc 1, knit to last 2 sts, inc 1, k1.
(10 sts)
Work 12 rows in stocking stitch.
Row 29: P1, p2tog, purl to last 3 sts,
p2togtbl, p1. (8 sts)
Row 30: K1, k2togtbl, knit to last 3 sts,
k2tog, k1. (6 sts)
Cast off.

Making up

For the mouth, stitch half of the mouth piece to the mouth end (cast-off end) of the underbody and top body pieces. Partially sew the two body pieces together using mattress stitch or backstitch, insert stuffing and complete the seam.

Using picture as guide, glue eyes to the head section.

To make the teeth, cut a strip of white felt, measure around the mouth, cut the strip to size, make evenly spaced diagonal cuts along one edge – first in one direction then in the other – to create teeth.

Using sewing thread, attach the teeth to the upper and lower jaw.

For the hat, use the hat pattern from Ha Pea Christmas (page 8) or Ho, Ho, Ho (page 26) or make a hat from felt.

BAA HUMBUG

Materials

To make one sheep:
* Yarn such as:
  Wendy Mode Aran, approx. 200m/
  100g ball (50% acrylic, 50% wool)
  1 ball in White 201
  1 ball in Black 220
* One pair of 4.5mm needles
* Tapestry needle
* Toy filling
* Short lengths of pink and red yarn
* One pair of 10mm wiggle eyes
* PVA glue or a glue gun
* One brown craft pipe cleaners
* One red craft pipe cleaner
* Two white craft pompoms

Tension

18 stitches and 22 rows over 10cm
stocking stitch.

Body and head (make 1)

Using 4.5mm needles and white yarn,
cast on 7 sts.
Row 1 (RS): Knit.
Row 2: [Inc 1 knitwise] 7 times. (14 sts)
Row 3: Knit.
Row 4: [Inc 1 knitwise] 14 times. (28 sts)
Work 14 rows in garter stitch.
Row 19: K1, k2togtbl, knit to the last
3 sts, k2tog, k1. (26 sts)
Repeat the last row 6 times more.
(14 sts)

Break off white yarn, join black yarn.
Starting with a knit row, work 6 rows
in stocking stitch.
Row 32: K1, [k2tog, k1] 4 times, k1.
(10 sts)
Row 33: Purl.
Row 34: [K1, k2tog] 3 times, k1. (7 sts)
Row 35: Purl.
Row 36: [K2tog] 3 times, k1. (4 sts)
Break off yarn and thread through
stitches on needle.
Draw tight and secure the end.

Tail (make 1)

Using 4.5mm needles and white yarn,
cast on 4 sts.
Work 10 rows in stocking stitch.
Cast off.

Ears (make 2)

Using 4.5mm needles and black yarn,
cast on 4 sts.
Work 10 rows in garter stitch.
Break off yarn and thread through
stitches on needle.
Draw tight and secure the end.

Legs (make 4)

Using 4.5mm needles and black yarn,
cast on 4 sts.
Work 8 rows in stocking stitch.
Cast off.

Making up

For the body and head, partially sew
up side seam, using mattress stitch
or backstitch, insert stuffing and
complete the seam.
Using picture as guide, attach ears and
tail then embroider nose using satin
stitch, using glue, attach the eyes.
For the legs, cut a length of pipe
cleaner to match the length of the
piece, sew up the seam around the
pipe cleaner, shape and attach to
the body.
To make a pair of antlers, twist and cut
a craft pipe cleaner to shape and glue
to head.
To make the earmuffs, use a short
length of craft pipe cleaner and attach
two small pompoms.
For the hat, use the hat pattern from
Ha Pea Christmas (page 8) or Ho, Ho,
Ho (page 26) or make a hat from felt.

THREE FRENCH HENS

Materials

To make one French hen:

* Yarn such as:
  Patons Fab DK, approx. 68m/25g
  ball (100% acrylic)
  1 ball in Yellow 2305
  1 ball in White 2306
  1 ball in Blue 2321 or Black 2311 (CC)
  1 ball in Orange 2333
  1 ball in Red 2322
* One pair of 3.75mm needles
* Stitch holder or safety pin
* Tapestry needle
* Toy filling
* One pair of 5mm wiggle eyes
* PVA glue or a glue gun

Tension

22 stitches and 26 rows over 10cm
stocking stitch.

Body and head (make 1)

Using 3.75mm needles and yellow yarn,
cast on 6 sts.
Row 1 (WS): Purl.
Row 2: [Inc 1 knitwise] 6 times. (12 sts)
Row 3: [Inc 1 purlwise] 12 times. (24 sts)
Row 4: [Inc 1, k1] 12 times. (36 sts)
Work 9 rows in stocking stitch.
Break off yellow yarn, join in white.
Row 14: [K1, p1] to end.
Work 3 rows more in rib pattern set
Join in CC yarn.
Work 10 rows in stocking stitch four
row stripe pattern as follows: * 2 rows
in CC yarn followed by 2 rows in white

yarn; repeat from * until end of section.
Row 28: K2, [k2tog, k3] 6 times, k2tog,
k2. (29 sts)
Row 29: Purl.
Row 30: K1, [k2tog, k2] 6 times, k2tog,
k2. (22 sts)
Row 31: Purl.
Row 32: [K2tog, k1] 6 times, k2tog, k2.
(15 sts)
Row 33: [P2tog] 7 times, k1. (8 sts)
Break off blue and white yarn, join in
yellow.
Row 34: [Inc 1] 8 times. (16 sts)
Row 35: Purl.
Row 36: [Inc 1, k1] 8 times. (24 sts)
Work 7 rows in stocking stitch.
Row 44: K1, [k2tog, k2] 5 times, k2tog,
k1. (18 sts)
Row 45: Purl.
Row 46: K1, [k2tog, k1] 5 times, k2tog.
(12 sts)
Row 47: Purl.
Row 48: [K2tog] 6 times. (6 sts)
Row 49: Purl.
Break off yarn and thread through
stitches on needle.
Draw tight and secure the end.

Wings (make 2)

Using 3.75mm needles and yellow yarn,
cast on 3 sts.
Row 1 (WS): Purl.
Row 2: [Inc 1] twice, k1. (5 sts)
Row 3: Purl.
Row 4: Inc 1, knit to the last 2 sts, inc 1,
k1. (7 sts)

Row 5: Purl.
Repeat the last 2 rows twice more.
(11 sts)
Work 10 rows in stocking stitch.
Break off yarn and thread through
stitches on needle.
Draw tight and secure the end.

Beak (make 1)

Using 3.75mm needles and orange
yarn, cast on 7 sts.
Work 2 rows in garter stitch.
Row 3: K2togtbl, knit to the last 2 sts,
k2tog. (5 sts)
Repeat the last row once more. (3 sts)
Cast off.

Comb (make 1)

Using 3.75mm needles and red yarn,
cast on 13 sts.
Work 2 rows in garter stitch.
Row 3: K4, turn, transfer the unworked
9 sts onto a stitch holder. (4 sts)
Row 4: K2togtbl, k2. (3 sts)
Row 5: Knit.
Row 6: K2togtbl, k1. (2 sts)
Row 7: K2togtbl.
Fasten off.
Transfer 5 sts from the stitch holder
onto needle, rejoin yarn.
Row 3: Knit.
Row 4: K2togtbl, k1, k2tog. (3 sts)
Row 5: Knit.
Row 6: K2togtbl, k1. (2 sts)
Row 7: K2togtbl.
Fasten off.

Transfer the remaining 4 sts from the stitch holder onto needle, rejoin yarn.
Row 3: Knit.
Row 4: K2, k2tog. (3 sts)
Row 5: Knit.
Row 6: K2, k2tog. (2 sts)
Row 7: K2tog.
Fasten off.

Base

Using 3.75mm needles and yellow yarn, cast on 8 sts.
Row 1 (WS) (and every WS row): Purl.
Row 2: [Inc 1] 8 times. (16 sts)
Row 4: [Inc 1, k1] 8 times. (24 sts)
Row 6: [Inc 1, k2] 8 times. (32 sts)
Row 7: Purl.
Cast off.

Beret (make 1)

Using 3.75mm needles and black yarn, cast on 10 sts.
Row 1 (RS): [Inc 1 knitwise] 10 times. (20 sts)
Row 2: Knit.
Row 3: [Inc 1 knitwise] 20 times. (40 sts)
Work 2 rows in garter stitch.
Row 6: K2, [k2tog, k3] 7 times, k2tog, k1. (32 sts)
Row 7: K1, [k2tog, k2] 7 times, k2tog, k1. (24 sts)
Row 8: [K2tog, k1] 7 times, k2tog, k1. (16 sts)
Row 9: [K2tog] 8 times. (8 sts)
Row 10: [K2tog] 4 times. (4 sts)
Break off yarn and thread through stitches on needle.
Draw tight and secure the end.

Beret bobble (make 1)

Using 3.75mm needles and black yarn, cast on 4 sts.
Work 4 rows in garter stitch.
Break off yarn and thread through stitches on needle.
Draw tight and secure the end.

Making up

For the body and head, partially sew up side seam, using mattress stitch or backstitch, insert stuffing and complete the seam. For the base, sew up the side seam and stitch the base to the bottom of the body.
For the beak fold in half, side edge to side edge and sew together around the outer edge.
Using picture as guide and matching yarn attach beak, comb and wings; glue eyes to the head sections.
For the beret, sew the side seam and attach a bobble.
For the hat, use the hat pattern from Ha Pea Christmas (page 8) or Ho, Ho, Ho (page 26) or make a hat from felt.

HAPPY CHRISTMAS, DEER

Materials
* Yarn such as:
  Sirdar Country Style DK, approx.
  155m/50g ball (40% nylon, 30%wool,
  30% acrylic)
  1 ball in Light Brown 477
* One pair of 3.75mm needles
* Tapestry needle
* Toy filling
* Short length of red yarn
* One pair of 5mm wiggle eyes
* PVA glue or a glue gun
* One brown craft pipe cleaner
* A small piece of red felt

Tension
22 stitches and 26 rows over 10cm
stocking stitch.

Legs, body and head
Using 3.75mm needles and light brown
yarn, cast on 40 sts.
Work 10 rows in garter stitch.
Row 11: Cast off 10 sts, knit to the end.
(30 sts)
Row 12: Cast off 10 sts, knit to the end.
(20 sts)
Work 10 rows in garter stitch.
Row 23: Cast on 10 sts, knit to the end.
(30 sts)
Row 24: Cast on 10 sts, knit to the end.
(40 sts)
Work 10 rows in garter stitch.
Row 35: Cast off 10 sts, knit to the end.
(30 sts)
Row 36: Cast off 10 sts, knit to the end.
(20 sts)
Row 37: K10, inc 1, k9. (21 sts)
Row 38: K1, k2togtbl, k7, inc 1, k7,
k2tog, k1. (20 sts)
Row 39: K1, k2togtbl, k14, k2tog, k1.
(18 sts)
Row 40: K1, k2togtbl, k6, inc 1, k5,
k2tog, k1. (17 sts)
Row 41: K1, k2togtbl, k11, k2tog, k1.
(15 sts)
Work 4 rows in garter stitch.
Row 46: Inc 1, k12, inc 1, k1. (17 sts)
Work 4 rows in garter stitch.
Row 51: K1 [k2tog] 8 times. (9 st)
Row 52: K1 [k2tog] 4 times. (5 st)
Leaving a long end break off yarn and
thread through stitches on needle.
Draw tight and secure the end.

Ears (make 2)
Using 3.75mm needles and light brown
yarn, cast on 5 sts.
Work 3 rows in garter stitch.
Break off yarn and thread through
stitches on needle.
Draw tight and secure the end.

Tail
Using 3.75mm needles and light brown
yarn, cast on 4 sts.
Work 5 rows in garter stitch.
Break off yarn and thread through
stitches on needle.
Draw tight and secure the end.

Making up
For the legs body and head, fold each
leg in half and sew up side seam, using
mattress stitch or backstitch, insert
stuffing and pipe cleaner. Using the
cast-off yarn end, sew up the body and
head side seam, insert stuffing and
complete the seam.
Using picture as guide, attach ears and
tail then embroider nose using satin
stitch, using glue, attach the eyes.
To make a pair of antlers, twist and cut
a craft pipe cleaner to shape and glue
to head.
To make the scarf, cut a strip of red felt
and make short cuts along the shorter
ends for the fringe.

HO HO HO

Materials

- Yarn such as:
  Patons Fab DK, approx. 68m/25g
  ball (100% acrylic)
  1 ball in Black 2311
  1 ball in White 2306
  1 ball in Red 2323
  1 ball in Skin 2328
- One pair of 3.75mm needles
- Tapestry needle
- Stitch holder
- Toy filling
- One pair of 5mm wiggle eyes
- Small pink craft pompom
- Small pieces of black felt
- Small gold buckle
- PVA glue or a glue gun

Tension

22 stitches and 26 rows over 10cm
stocking stitch.

Legs (make 2)

*Using 3.75mm needles and black yarn,
cast on 8 sts.
Row 1 (WS): Purl.
Row 2: [Inc 1 knitwise] 8 times.
(16 sts)
Work 8 rows in stocking stitch.
Break off black yarn, join in white.
Work 2 rows in stocking stitch.
Break off white yarn, join in red.
Work 12 rows in stocking stitch.
Cast off.

Body and head

Using 3.75mm needles and red yarn,
cast on 32 sts.
Starting with a knit row, work 12 rows
in stocking stitch.
Row 13: K1, [k2tog, k4] 5 times, k1.
(27 sts)
Row 14: Purl.
Row 15: K1, [k2tog, k3] 5 times, k1.
(22 sts)
Row 16: Purl.
Row 17: K1, [k2tog, k2] 5 times, k1.
(17 sts)
Row 18: Purl.
Row 19: K1, [k2tog, k1] 5 times, k1.
(12 sts)
Break off red yarn, join in skin.
Work 2 rows in stocking stitch.
Row 22: [Inc 1, p1] 6 times. (18 sts)
Work 11 rows in stocking stitch.
Row 34: [P2tog] 9 times. (9 sts)
Break off yarn and thread through
stitches on needle.
Draw tight and secure the end.

Jacket

Using 3.75mm needles and white yarn,
cast on 38 sts.
Starting with a knit row, work 2 rows
in stocking stitch.
Break off white yarn, join in red.
Work 10 rows in stocking stitch.
Break off red yarn, join in black.
Work 2 rows in garter stitch.
Cast off.

Arms (make 2)

Using 3.75mm needles and red yarn,
cast on 10 sts.
Starting with a knit row, work 16 rows
in stocking stitch.
Break off red yarn, join in white.
Work 2 rows in stocking stitch.
Break off white yarn, join in skin.
Row 19: [K2tog] 5 times. (5 sts)
Row 20: Purl.
Break off yarn and thread through
stitches on needle.
Draw tight and secure the end.

Beard

Using 3.75mm needles and white yarn,
cast on 15 sts.
Work 4 rows in garter stitch.
Row 5: K2togtbl, knit to the last
2 sts, k2tog. (13 sts)
Row 6: Knit.
Repeat last 2 rows 5 times more.
(3 sts)
Row 17: Slip 1 st, k2tog, psso.
Break off yarn and fasten off.

Fringe

Using 3.75mm needles and white yarn,
cast on 9 sts.
Row 1: K2togtbl, knit to the last 2 sts,
k2tog. (7 sts)
Repeat the last row once more. (5 sts)
Cast off.

Hat

Using 3.75mm needles and white yarn, cast on 26 sts.

Starting with a knit row, work 2 rows in stocking stitch.

Break off white yarn, join in red.

Work 2 rows in stocking stitch.

Row 5: [K5, k2tog] 3 times, k5. (23 sts)

Row 6: Purl.

Row 7: [K4, k2tog] 3 times, k5. (20 sts)

Row 8: Purl.

Row 9: K4 [k2tog, k3] twice, k2tog, k4. (17 sts)

Row 10: Purl.

Row 11: K3 [k2tog, k2] twice, k2tog, k4. (14 sts)

Row 12: Purl.

Row 13: K3 [k2tog, k1] twice, k2tog, k3. (11 sts)

Row 14: Purl.

Row 15: K1, [k2tog] 5 times. (6 sts)

Row 16: Purl.

Break off yarn and thread through stitches on needle.

Draw tight and secure the end.

Bobble

Using 3.75mm needles and white yarn, cast on 5 sts.

Work 3 rows In garter stitch.

Break off yarn and thread through stitches on needle.

Draw tight and secure the end.

Making up

For the body and head, partially sew up back seam, using mattress stitch or backstitch, insert stuffing and complete the seam.

For the arms and legs, fold the each piece in half sew up side seam, insert toy stuffing.

Wrap the jacket around the body section and stitch in place.

Using matching yarn, sew up the side seam of the hat and attach the bobble.

Attach the beard, fringe and hat to the head.

Using picture as guide and glue attach eyes and small pompom to the head section and the buckle to the belt.

HAVE AN ICE CHRISTMAS

Materials

* Yarn such as:
  Patons Fab DK, approx. 274m/100g ball (100% acrylic)
  1 ball in White 2306
  Patons Fab DK, approx. 68m/25g ball (100% acrylic)
  1 ball in Black 2311
  1 ball in Red 2323
* One pair of 3.75mm needles
* Tapestry needle
* Toy filling
* One pair of 10mm wiggle eyes
* PVA glue or a glue gun
* Small amount of white felt
* Sewing needle and matching thread
* A pair of toy ice skates

Tension

22 stitches and 30 rows over 10cm stocking stitch.

Head and body

Using 3.75mm needles and black yarn, cast on 4 sts.
Row 1 (RS): [Inc 1 knitwise] 4 times. (8 sts)
Row 2: Purl.
Row 3: [Inc 1, k1] 4 times. (12 sts)
Row 4: Purl.
Break off black yarn, join in white.
Row 5: [Inc 1 knitwise] 12 times. (24 sts)
Row 6: Purl.
Row 7: K8, inc 1, k6, inc 1, k8. (26 sts)
Row 8: P8, inc 1, p8, inc 1, p8. (28 sts)
Row 9: K8, inc 1, k10, inc 1, k8. (30 sts)
Row 10: P8, inc 1, p12, inc 1, p8. (32 sts)
Row 11: K8, inc 1, k14, inc 1, k8. (34 sts)
Row 12: P8, inc 1, p16, inc 1, p8. (36 sts)
Row 13: K8, inc 1, k18, inc 1, k8. (38 sts)
Row 14: P8, inc 1, p20, inc 1, p8. (40 sts)
Row 15: Inc 1, k7, inc 1, k22, inc 1, k7, inc 1. (44 sts)
Row 16: P9, inc 1, p24, inc 1, p9. (46 sts)
Row 17: Inc 1, k8, inc 1, k26, inc 1, k8, inc 1. (50 sts)
Row 18: P10, inc 1, p28, inc 1, p10. (52 sts)

First ear

Short or partial rows of stitches are worked as follows.
Row 19: K17, turn and work on first 7 sts (to form first ear).
*Row 20: P7, turn.
Row 21: K7, turn.
Row 22: P7, turn.
Row 23: K2tog, k3, k2tog, turn. (5 sts)
Row 24: P5, turn.
Row 25: K5, turn.
Row 26: P5, turn.
Row 27: K2tog, k1, k2tog, turn. (3 sts)
Row 28: P3, turn.
Row 29: K3, turn.
Row 30: P3, turn.
Row 31: K3, turn.

Row 32: P3, turn.
Row 33: Inc 1, k1, inc 1, turn. (5 sts)
Row 34: P5, turn.
Row 35: K5, turn.
Row 36: P5, turn.
Row 37: Inc 1, k3, inc 1, turn. (7 sts)
Row 38: P7, turn.
Row 39: K7, turn.
Row 40: P7, turn.

Second ear

Row 41: K7 (sts from first ear), k25, turn and work on first 7 sts (to form second ear), work from * to row 40; then complete row 41 as follows:
K7 (sts from second ear), k10. (52 sts)

Neck and upper body

Row 42: Inc 1, p17, p2tog, p12, p2tog, p17, inc 1.
Row 43: Inc 1, k17, k2tog, k12, k2tog, k17, inc 1.
Repeat last 2 rows 5 times more.
Row 54: Inc 1, p17, p2tog, p12, p2tog, p17, inc 1.
Row 55: Inc 1, knit to the last 2 sts, inc 1, k1. (54 sts)
Work 3 rows in stocking stitch.
Repeat last 4 rows 3 times more. (60 sts)

Front legs

Row 71: Cast on 15 sts, knit to end. (75 sts)
Row 72: Cast on 15 sts, purl to end. (90 sts)
Work 16 rows in stocking stitch.
Row 89: Cast off 15 sts, knit to end. (75 sts)
Row 90: Cast off 15 sts, purl to end. (60 sts)
Work 10 rows in stocking stitch.

Back legs

Row 101: Cast on 15 sts, knit to end. (75 sts)
Row 102: Cast on 15 sts, purl to end. (90 sts)
Row 103: K42, k2tog, k2, k2tog, k42. (88 sts)
Row 104: Purl.
Row 105: K41, k2tog, k2, k2tog, k41. (86 sts)
Row 106: Purl.
Row 107: K40, k2tog, k2, k2tog, k40. (84 sts)
Row 108: Purl.
Row 109: K39, k2tog, k2, k2tog, k39. (82 sts)
Row 110: Purl.
Row 111: K38, k2tog, k2, k2tog, k38. (80 sts)
Row 112: Purl.
Row 113: K37, k2tog, k2, k2tog, k37. (78 sts)
Row 114: Purl.
Row 115: K36, k2tog, k2, k2tog, k36. (76 sts)
Row 116: Purl.
Row 117: K35, k2tog, k2, k2tog, k35. (74 sts)
Row 118: Purl.
Row 119: K34, k2tog, k2, k2tog, k34. (72 sts)
Row 120: Purl.
Cast off.

Tummy

Using 3.75mm needles and white yarn, cast on 3 sts.
Row 1 (WS): Purl.
Row 2: [Inc 1] twice, k1. (5 sts)
Row 3: Purl.
Row 4: Inc 1, knit to the last 2 sts, inc 1, k1. (7 sts)
Row 5: Purl.
Repeat the last 2 rows 6 more times. (19 sts)
Work 8 rows in stocking stitch.
Row 26: K1, k2togtbl, knit to the last 3 sts, k2tog, k1. (17 sts)
Row 27: Purl.
Repeat the last 2 rows 7 more times. (3 sts)
Cast off.

Scarf

Using 3.75mm needles and red yarn, cast on 9 sts.
Work in garter stitch until work measures 36cm.
Cast off.

Making up

Fold the ears in half and sew up the side seam using mattress stitch or back stitch. For the head, body and tummy, fold the legs in half and stitch the edges together, pin the tummy in place and partially sew up the seam, insert stuffing and complete the seam.
Using picture as guide, and using glue, attach the eyes.
For the feet, cut small circles of felt approximately 20mm in diameter and using sewing thread stitch in place. Add a fringe to the short edges of the scarf. For the hat, use the hat pattern from Ha Pea Christmas (page 8) or Ho, Ho, Ho (page 26). Attach toy ice skates.

PENGUIN

Materials

※ Yarn such as:
    Sirdar Toytime DK Bonus, approx.
    70m/25g ball (100% acrylic)
    1 ball in Black 965
    1 ball in White 961
    1 ball in Orange 981
    Anchor Artiste Metallic, approx.
    250m/25g ball (80% Viscose,
    20% Metallised Polyester)
    1 ball in Silver 301
※ One pair of 3.75mm needles
※ One pair of 3.25mm needles
※ Stitch holder
※ Tapestry needle
※ Toy filling
※ One pair of 10mm wiggle eyes
※ PVA glue or a glue gun
※ One pink craft pipe cleaner
※ Two pink craft pompoms
※ Card

Tension

Using Patons Fab DK and 3.75mm
needles 22 stitches and 26 rows over
10cm stocking stitch.

Body and head

Using 3.75mm needles and black yarn,
cast on 12 sts.
Row 1 (WS): Purl.
Row 2: [Inc 1] 12 times. (24 sts)
Row 3: Purl.
Row 4: [Inc 1, k1] 12 times. (36 sts)
Work 25 rows in stocking stitch.
Row 30: [K1, k2tog] 12 times. (24 sts)

Work 11 rows in stocking stitch.
Row 42: [K2tog] 12 times. (12 sts)
Row 43: [P2tog] 6 times. (6 sts)
Break off yarn and thread through stitches on needle.
Draw tight and secure the end.

White bib

Using 3.75mm needles and white yarn, cast on 4 sts.
Row 1 (RS): Inc 1, knit to last st, inc 1. (6 sts)
Row 2: Inc 1, purl to last st, inc 1. (8 sts)
Repeat the last 2 rows 4 times more. (16 sts)
Work 14 rows in stocking stitch.
Row 25: [K2tog] 8 times. (8 sts)
Row 26: Inc 1, purl to last 2 sts, inc 1, p1. (10 sts)
Row 27: Inc 1, knit to last 2 sts, inc 1, k1. (12 sts)
Row 28: Inc 1, purl to last 2 sts, inc 1, p1. (14 sts)

Right eye lobe

Row 29: K5, k2tog, transfer the rem 7 sts onto a stitch holder. (6 sts)
Row 30: P2tog, p2, p2tog. (4 sts)
Row 31: K2togtbl, k2tog. (2 sts)
Cast off.

Left eye lobe

Transfer stitches from stitch holder onto the needle and rejoin yarn.
Row 29: Sl1, k1 psso, k5. (6 sts)
Work as Right eye lobe rows 30–31.
Cast off.

Feet

Using 3.75mm needles and orange yarn, cast on 8 sts.
Row 1 (RS): Inc 1, k to the last 2 sts, inc 1, k1. (10 sts)
Repeat the last row twice more. (14 sts)

Right foot

Row 4: Inc 1, k4, k2tog, transfer the rem 7 sts onto a stitch holder. (7 sts)
Row 5: K1, k2tog, knit to end. (6 sts)
Row 6: K1, [k2tog] twice, k1. (4 sts)
Cast off.

Left foot

Transfer stitches from stitch holder onto the needle and rejoin yarn.
Row 4: Sl1, k1, psso, k3, inc 1, k1. (7 sts)
Work as Right foot rows 5–6.

Beak

Using 3.75mm needles and orange yarn, cast on 2 sts.
Row 1 (RS): [Inc 1] twice. (4 sts)
Row 2: Inc 1, k to the last 2 sts, inc 1, k1. (6 sts)
Repeat the last row 3 times more. (12 sts)
Work 2 rows in garter stitch.
Cast off.

Outer wing (make 2)

Using 3.75mm needles and black yarn, cast on 8 sts.
Row 1 (WS): Purl.
Row 2: Inc 1, k to the last 2 sts, inc 1, k1. (10 sts)
Repeat the last 2 rows once more. (12 sts)
Work 5 rows in stocking stitch.
Row 10: K1, k2togtbl, knit to last 3 sts, k2tog, k1. (10 sts)
Row 11: Purl.

Repeat the last 2 rows 4 times more. (2 sts)
Cast off.

Inner wings (make 2)

Using 3.75mm needles and white yarn, cast on 8 sts.
Work as for Outer wings.

Scarf

Using 3.25mm needles and silver metallic yarn, cast on 7 sts.
Work in garter stitch until work measures 36cm.
Cast off.

Making up

For the body and head, partially sew up side seam, using mattress stitch or backstitch, insert stuffing and complete the seam. Attach the white bib. For beak, fold the beak in half and, starting from the tip, sew together from cast-on edge to cast-off edge. For wings, with the stocking stitch side facing outwards, sew the two pieces together, using mattress stitch or backstitch, around the edge.
Draw around the feet onto thin card and stitch the card to the base of the feet.
Using picture as a guide, attach the beak, wings and feet and, using glue, attach the eyes.
Add a fringe to the short edges of the scarf.
To make the earmuffs, use a short length of craft pipe cleaner and attach two small pompoms.

WE THREE KINGS

Materials

To make one king:

* Yarn such as:
  Patons Fab DK, approx. 68m/25g
  ball (100% acrylic)
  1 ball in Skin 2328
  For the tunic, 1 ball in either:
  Red 2323; Navy 2320; Green 2319.
  Anchor Artiste Metallic, approx.
  250m/25g ball (80% Viscose,
  20% Metallised Polyester) to match
  the tunic colours above.
  1 ball in either:
  Red 318; Navy 321; Green 322.
  Sirdar Funky Fur approx. 90m/50g
  ball (100% polyester)
  1 ball in Black 510
* One pair of 3.75mm needles
* One pair of 3.25mm needles
* Tapestry needle
* One inner cardboard roll from rolls
  of kitchen towel
* One pair of 10mm wiggle eyes
* Short length of pink embroidery
  thread
* Plastic craft jewels
* Paper-clip style jewel fasteners
* Small amount of gold thin card
* Small amount of gold paper

Tension

Using Patons Fab DK and 3.75mm
needles 22 stitches and 26 rows over
10cm stocking stitch.

Body and head

Using 3.75mm needles and yarn for
tunic, cast on 32 sts.
Work 4 rows in stocking stitch.
Row 5: K1, k2togtbl, knit to the last
3 sts, k2tog, k1. (30 sts)
Work 3 rows in stocking stitch.
Repeat the last 4 rows 7 times more.
(16 sts)
Break off tunic yarn, join in skin.
Row 37: Knit.
Row 38: [P2tog] 8 times. (8 sts)
Row 39: [K2tog] 4 times. (4 sts)
Row 40: [Inc 1] 4 times. (8 sts)
Row 41: [Inc 1 knitwise] 8 times. (16 sts)
Row 42: [Inc 1, p1] 8 times. (24 sts)
Work 14 rows of stocking stitch.
Row 57: [K2tog] 12 times. (12 sts)
Row 58: [P2tog] 6 times. (6 sts)
Break off yarn and thread through
stitches on needle.
Draw tight and secure the end.

Arms (make 2)

Using 3.75mm needles and tunic yarn,
cast on 10 sts.
Work 16 rows in stocking stitch.
Break off tunic yarn, join in skin.
Work 5 rows in stocking stitch.
Row 22: [P2tog] 5 times. (5 sts)
Break off yarn and thread through
stitches on needle.
Draw tight and secure the end.

Base

Using 3.75mm needles and tunic yarn,
cast on 8 sts.
Row 1 (WS) (and every WS row): Purl.
Row 2: [Inc 1] 8 times. (16 sts)
Row 4: [Inc 1, k1] 8 times. (24 sts)
Row 6: K1, [inc 1, k2] 7 times, inc 1, k1.
(32 sts)
Row 7: Purl.
Cast off.

Cloak

Using 3.25mm needles and metallic
yarn, cast on 50 sts.
Work 4 rows in garter stitch.
Work 30 rows in stocking stitch.
Row 35: [K2tog] 25 times. (25 sts)
Work 4 rows in garter stitch.
Cast off.

Making up

For the body and head, sew up side
seam, using mattress stitch or
backstitch. Insert an inner cardboard
roll from a roll of toilet tissue and
insert stuffing. For the base, sew up
the side seam and stitch the base to
the bottom of the body.
Using picture as guide, for the hair,
working from crown outwards, coil
and stitch in place the fur yarn to the
top of the head; embroider the mouth
using backstitch; using glue attach
eyes to the head section.
Attach the arms to the body and head.
Use the gold card to make a crown to

fit the head and the gold fabric or
tissue to create the fabric cap.
Using glue or fastening provided to
attach craft jewels.
Make gifts from gold card, craft jewels
and gold fabric and tissue.

CHRIS MOOSE

Materials

* Yarn such as:
  Sirdar Country Style DK, approx.
  155m/50g ball (40% nylon, 30%wool,
  30% acrylic)
  1 ball in Light Brown 964
  1 ball in Brown 947
* One pair of 3.75mm needles
* Tapestry needle
* Toy filling
* One pair of 15mm wiggle eyes
* PVA glue or a glue gun
* One brown craft pipe cleaner
* A small piece of brown felt
* A small piece of thin card
* A short length of red yarn

Tension

22 stitches and 30 rows over 10cm
stocking stitch.

Body

Using 3.75mm needles and light brown
yarn, cast on 12 sts.
Row 1 (WS): Purl.
Row 2: [Inc 1 knitwise] 12 times. (24 sts)
Row 3: Purl.
Row 4: [Inc 1 knitwise] 24 times.
(48 sts)
Work 29 rows in stocking stitch.
Row 34: [K2tog] 24 times. (24 sts)
Row 35: Purl.
Row 36: [K2tog] 12 times. (12 sts)
Row 37: Purl.
Row 38: [K2tog] 6 times. (6 sts)
Row 39: Purl.

Break off yarn and thread through
stitches on needle.
Draw tight and secure the end.

Head

Using 3.75mm needles and light brown
yarn, cast on 6 sts.
Row 1 (WS): Purl.
Row 2: [Inc 1 knitwise] 6 times. (12 sts)
Row 3: Purl.
Row 4: [Inc 1 knitwise] 12 times.
(24 sts)
Work 7 rows in stocking stitch.
Row 12: [K2tog] 12 times. (12 sts)
Row 13: Purl.
Row 14: [Inc 1, k1] 6 times. (18 sts)
Work 7 rows in stocking stitch.
Row 22: [K2tog] 9 times. (9 sts)
Row 23: [P2tog] 4 times, k1. (5 sts)
Row 24: Purl.
Break off yarn and thread through
stitches on needle.
Draw tight and secure the end.

Legs (make 4)

Using 3.75mm needles and light brown
yarn, cast on 12 sts.
Work 12 rows in stocking stitch.
Break off light brown yarn, join in
brown.
Work 4 rows in stocking stitch.
Row 17: [K2tog] 6 times. (6 sts)
Break off yarn and thread through
stitches on needle.
Draw tight and secure the end.

Tail

Using 3.75mm needles and light brown
yarn, cast on 6 sts.
Work 4 rows in garter stitch.
Break off yarn and thread through
stitches on needle.
Draw tight and secure the end.

Ears (make 2)

Using 3.75mm needles and light brown
yarn, cast on 5 sts.
Work 3 rows in garter stitch.
Break off yarn and thread through
stitches on needle.
Draw tight and secure the end.

Making up

For the body and head pieces, partially
sew up side seams, using mattress
stitch or backstitch, insert stuffing
and complete the seams. Using picture
as guide, attach ears and tail then
embroider nose using brown yarn
and straight stitch, using glue, attach
the eyes. For the legs, cut a length of
pipe cleaner to match the length of the
piece, sew up the seam around the
pipe cleaner, shape and attach to
the body.
To make a pair of antlers, cut antler
shapes from felt, twist a craft pipe
cleaner to the same shape to support
the felt, glue the felt to the pipe
cleaner and glue to head.
Make a sign from a small piece of thin
card and a scrap of red yarn.

ANGEL

Materials

* ❊ Yarn such as:
  Patons Fab DK, approx. 68m/25g ball (100% acrylic)
  1 ball in White 2306
  1 ball in Skin 2328
  Anchor Artiste Metallic, approx. 250m/25g ball (80% Viscose, 20% Metallised Polyester)
  1 ball in Silver 301
* ❊ One pair of 3.25mm needles
* ❊ Stitch holder
* ❊ Tapestry needle
* ❊ One pair of 5mm wiggle eyes
* ❊ Short length of pink embroidery thread
* ❊ One silver craft pipe cleaner
* ❊ A small piece of organza fabric

Tension

Using Patons Fab DK and 3.25mm needles 18 stitches and 22 rows over 10cm stocking stitch.

Body and head

Front

Using 3.25mm needles and silver metallic yarn, cast on 31 sts.
*Starting with a knit row, work 2 rows of stocking stitch.
Row 3: K1, k2togtbl, knit to the last 3 sts, k2tog, k1. (29 sts)
Work 3 rows of stocking stitch.
Row 7: K1, k2togtbl, knit to the last 3 sts, k2tog, k1. (27 sts)
Repeat the last 4 rows 10 times more. (7 sts)
Work 2 rows of stocking stitch.*
Break yarn and transfer stitches onto stitch holder.

Back

Using 3.25mm needles and white yarn, cast on 31 sts.
Repeat from * to *.
Break off white yarn, join in skin yarn.

Head

Row 50: Inc 1, p5, inc 1 (sts from back), inc 1, p5, inc 1 (sts from front). (18 sts)
Row 51: [Inc 1, k2] 6 times. (24 sts)
Work 9 rows of stocking stitch.
Row 61: [K2tog] 12 times. (12 sts)
Row 62: [P2tog] 6 times. (6 sts)
Row 63: [K2tog] 3 times. (3 sts)
Break off yarn and thread through stitches on needle.
Draw tight and secure the end.

Arms (make 2)

Using 3.25mm needles and silver metallic yarn, cast on 12 sts.
Work 16 rows of stocking stitch.
Break off silver metallic yarn, join in skin yarn.
Row 17: [K2tog] 6 times. (6 sts)
Work 3 rows of stocking stitch.
Row 21: [K2tog] 3 times. (3 sts)
Break off yarn and thread through stitches on needle.
Draw tight and secure the end.

Base

Using 3.25mm needles and white yarn, cast on 8 sts.
Row 1 (WS)(and every WS row): Purl.
Row 2: [Inc 1] 8 times. (16 sts)
Row 4: [Inc 1, k1] 8 times. (24 sts)
Row 6: K1, [inc 1, k2] 7 times, inc 1, k1. (32 sts)
Row7: Purl.
Cast off.

Making up

For the body and head, sew up side seam, using mattress stitch or backstitch and insert stuffing.

For the base, sew up the side seam and stitch the base to the bottom of the body.

Using picture as guide, for the hair, using white yarn and leaving a long yarn tail, work a small back stitch into the head, cut the yarn a distance equal to the yarn tail from the stitch. Repeat randomly over the head section.

Embroider the mouth using backstitch; using glue attach eyes to the head section.

Attach the arms to the body and head and stitch the hands together.

For the wings, cut two butterfly wing shapes from the organza fabric – one for the upper wings, approximately 12cm wide, and one for the lower wings, approximately 10cm wide. Fold the wings in half and unfold. Place the upper wings on top of the lower wings, overlapping them by about 1cm and attach by stitching through the fold along the spine of the angel using silver yarn.

To make a necklace, wrap the pipe cleaner loosely around the neck of the angel, cut the pipe cleaner to size and twist to secure.

To make a halo, make a ring, 3cm in diameter, from the silver pipe cleaner. Attach a straight length to the ring and attach to the back of the head.

SNOWMAN

Materials

* Yarn such as:
  Sirdar Supersoft Aran approx.
  236m/100g ball (100% acrylic)
  1 ball in White 830
  Sirdar Toytime DK Bonus, approx.
  70m/25g ball (100% acrylic)
  1 ball in Orange 981
  1 ball in Red 977
  1 ball in Green 916
* One pair of 4.5mm needles
* One pair of 3.75mm needles
* Tapestry needle
* Toy filling
* Short length of black yarn
* PVA glue or a glue gun

Tension

Sirdar Supersoft Aran and 4.5mm
needles 18 stitches and 22 rows over
10cm stocking stitch.

Body and head

Using 4.5mm needles and white yarn,
cast on 30 sts.
Work 14 rows in stocking stitch.
Row 15 (RS): [K2, k2tog] 7 times, k2.
(23 sts)
Row 16: Purl.
Row 17: [K1, k2tog] 7 times, k2. (16 sts)
Row 18: Purl.
Row 19: [K2tog] 7 times, k2. (9 sts)
Row 20: Purl.
Row 21: [Inc 1 knitwise] 9 times. (18 sts)
Work 9 rows in stocking stitch.
Row 31: [K2tog] 9 times. (9 sts)

Row 32: Purl.
Row 33: [K2tog, k1] 3 times. (6 sts)
Break off yarn and thread through
stitches on needle.
Draw tight and secure the end.

Base

Using 4.5mm needles and white yarn,
cast on 8 sts.
Row 1 (WS)(and every WS row): Purl.
Row 2: [Inc 1] 8 times. (16 sts)
Row 4: [Inc 1, k1] 8 times. (24 sts)
Row 6: K1, [inc 1, k2] 7 times, inc 1, k1.
(32 sts)
Row 7: Purl.
Cast off.

Nose

Using 3.75mm needles and orange
yarn, cast on 5 sts.
Row 1: Knit.
Row 2: K2tog, k1, k2tog. (3 sts)
Row 3: Knit.
Row 4: Slip 1 st, k2tog, psso.
Break off yarn and thread through
stitches on needle.
Draw tight and secure the end.

Scarf

Using 3.75mm needles and red yarn,
cast on 7 sts.
Work 4 rows in garter stitch.
Join in green yarn.
Work 4 rows in garter stitch.
*Using red yarn, work 4 rows in garter
stitch.
Using green yarn, work 4 rows in
garter stitch.
Repeat from * 6 more times.
Cast off.

Making up

For the body and head, partially sew
up side seam, using mattress stitch
or backstitch, insert stuffing and
complete the seam.
For the base, sew up the side seam
and stitch the base to the bottom of
the body.
For the nose, fold in half, cast-on edge
to cast-off edge and sew together
around the outer edge.
Using picture as guide and matching
yarn, attach the beak and, embroider
the eyes and mouth using satin stitch.
Add a fringe to the short edges of
the scarf and wrap around the
snowman's neck.
For the hat, use the hat pattern from
Ha Pea Christmas (page 8) or Ho, Ho,
Ho (page 26) or make a hat from felt.

MISTLE TOAD AND WINE

Materials

※ Yarn such as:
Patons Fab DK, approx. 318m/100g ball (100% acrylic)
1 ball in Green 2341
Patons Fab DK, approx. 68m/25g ball (100% acrylic)
1 ball in Lime 2317
※ One pair of 3.75mm needles
※ Stitch holder
※ Tapestry needle
※ Toy filling
※ Short length of black yarn
※ One pair of 15mm wiggle eyes
※ PVA glue or a glue gun

Tension

21 stitches and 29 rows over 10cm stocking stitch.

Body and head (make 2)

Right leg piece

Using 3.75mm needles and lime yarn, cast on 3 sts.
Row 1 (WS): Purl.
Row 2: Inc 1, knit to end. (4 sts)
Row 3: Purl to last 2 sts, inc 1, p1. (5 sts)
Repeat last 2 rows 3 times more. (11 sts)
Row 10: Knit to last 2 sts, inc 1, k1. (12 sts)
Work 4 rows in stocking stitch.
Row 15: Cast off 6 sts, purl to end of row. (6 sts)
Break off lime yarn, join in green yarn.
Work 20 rows in stocking stitch.
Break off yarn and transfer stitches onto a stitch holder.

Left leg piece

Using 3.75mm needles and lime yarn, cast on 3 sts.
Row 1 (WS): Purl.
Row 2: Knit to last 2 sts, inc 1, k1. (4 sts)
Row 3: Inc 1, purl to end. (5 sts)
Repeat last 2 rows 3 times more. (11 sts)
Row 10: Knit to last 2 sts, inc 1, k1. (12 sts)
Work 3 rows in stocking stitch.
Row 14: Cast off 6 sts, knit to end of row. (6 sts)
Break off lime yarn, join in green yarn.
Work 21 rows in stocking stitch.
Break off yarn.

Body

Join the legs by working across the stitches of both legs as follows:
with the right side of the left leg facing and the needle tip to the right, transfer the stitches from the stitch holder, with right side facing, onto the same needle. Join in green yarn.
Row 36: Cast on 4 sts, knit across stitches of right leg piece, cast on 15 sts, knit across the left leg piece. (31 sts)
Row 37: Cast on 4 sts, purl to the end. (35 sts)
Work 4 rows in stocking stitch.
Row 42: Cast off 5 sts, knit to end (30 sts)
Row 43: Cast off 5 sts, purl to end (25 sts)
Work 2 rows in stocking stitch.
Row 46: K1, k2togtbl, knit to last 3 sts, k2tog, k1. (23 sts)
Work 3 rows in stocking stitch.
Repeat last 4 rows 4 times more. (15 sts)

Break off green yarn, join in lime yarn.
Work 2 rows in stocking stitch.
Break off lime yarn, join in green yarn.
Row 84: Inc 1, knit to last 2 sts, inc 1, k1. (17 sts)
Work 3 rows in stocking stitch.
Row 88: Inc 1, knit to last 2 sts, inc 1, k1. (19 sts)
Repeat last 4 rows once more. (21 sts)
Row 93: Purl.

Right eye

Row 94: K6, transfer the rem 15 sts onto a stitch holder. (6 sts)
Row 95: P1, p2tog, p2. (5 sts)
Row 96: K2, k2tog, k1. (4 sts)
Row 97: P1, p2tog, p1. (3 sts)
Row 98: Sl1, k2tog, psso.
Fasten off.

Left eye

Transfer stitches from stitch holder onto the needle and rejoin yarn.
Row 94: Cast off 9 sts, knit to end. (6 sts)
Row 95: P3, p2tog, p1. (5 sts)
Row 96: K1, k2tog, k2. (4 sts)
Row 97: P1, p2tog, p1. (3 sts)
Row 98: Sl1, k2tog, psso.
Fasten off.

Arms (make 4)

Using 3.75mm needles and green yarn, cast on 4 sts.
Starting with a knit row, work 2 rows in stocking stitch.
Row 3: Inc 1, knit to last 2 sts, inc 1, k1. (6 sts)

Work 13 rows in stocking stitch.
Break off green yarn, join in lime yarn.
Row 17. Knit.
Row 18: Inc 1, purl to last 2 sts, inc 1, k1.
(8 sts)
Row 19: Inc 1, knit to last 2 sts, inc 1, k1.
(10 sts)
Work 3 rows in stocking stitch.
Row 23: K1, sl1, k1 psso, k4, k2tog, k1.
(8 sts)
Row 24: P1, p2togtbl, p2, p2tog, p1. (6 sts)

Row 25: K1, sl1, k1 psso, k2tog, k1.
(4 sts)
Row 26: P2togtbl, p2tog. (2 sts)
Work 2 rows in stocking stitch.
Cast off.

Making up
For the body and head, partially sew
the two pieces together using
mattress stitch or backstitch, insert
stuffing and complete the seam.

Repeat with each arm.
Using picture as guide, embroider the
mouth using backstitch and, using
glue, attach eyes to the head section.
For the hat, use the hat pattern from
Ha Pea Christmas (page 8) or Ho, Ho,
Ho (page 26) or make a hat from felt.

KNITTING BASICS

WORKING FROM A PATTERN

Before starting any pattern, always read it through. This will give you an idea of how the design is structured and the techniques that are involved. Each pattern includes the following basic elements:

Materials

This section gives a list of materials required, including the amount of yarn, the sizes of needles and extras.

Abbreviations

Knitting instructions are normally given in an abbreviated form, which saves valuable space. In this book the abbreviations are listed on page 48.

Project instructions

Before starting to knit, read the instructions carefully to understand the abbreviations used, how the design is structured and in which order each piece is worked. However, there may be some parts of the pattern that only become clear when you are knitting them, so do not assume that you are being slow or that the pattern is wrong.

Tension (gauge) and selecting correct needle size

Tension (gauge) can differ quite dramatically between knitters. This is because of the way that the needles and the yarn are held. So if your tension (gauge) does not match that stated in the pattern, you should change your needle size following this simple rule:

❋　If your knitting is too loose, your tension (gauge) will read that you have fewer stitches and rows than the given tension (gauge), and you will need to change to a smaller needle to make the stitch size smaller.

❋　If your knitting is too tight, your tension (gauge) will read that you have more stitches and rows than the given tension (gauge), and you will need to change to a thicker needle to make the stitch size bigger.

Making up

The Making up section in each project will tell you how to join the knitted pieces together. Always follow the recommended sequence.

KNITTING A TENSION SWATCH

No matter how excited you are about a new knitting project and how annoying it seems to have to spend time knitting a tension swatch before you start, please do take the time, as it will not be wasted.

Use the same needles, yarn and stitch pattern as those that will be used for the main work and knit a sample at least 12.5cm (5in) square. Smooth out the finished piece on a flat surface, but do not stretch it.

To check the stitch tension, place a ruler horizontally on the sample, measure 10cm (4in) across and mark with a pin at each end. Count the number of stitches between the pins. To check the row tension, place a ruler vertically on the sample, measure 10cm (4in) and mark with pins. Count the number of rows between the pins. If the number of stitches and rows is greater then specified in the pattern, make a new swatch using larger needles; if it is less, make a new swatch using smaller needles.

MAKING A SLIP KNOT

A slip knot is the basis of all casting-on techniques and is therefore the starting point for almost everything you do in knitting.

1   Wind the yarn around two fingers twice, as shown. Insert a knitting needle through the first (front) strand and under the second (back) one.

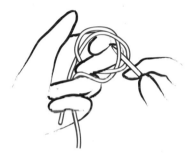

2   Using the needle, pull the back strand through the front one to form a loop. Holding the loose ends of the yarn with your left hand, pull the needle upwards, thus tightening the knot.

CASTING ON

Casting on is the term used for making a row of stitches to be used as a foundation for your knitting.

1   Place the slip knot on the needle, leaving a long tail, and hold the needle in your right hand.

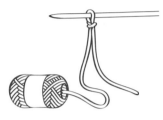

2   * Wind the loose end of the yarn around your thumb from front to back. Place the ball end of the yarn over your left forefinger.

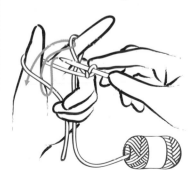

3   Insert the point of the needle under the loop on your thumb. With your right index finger, take the ball end of the yarn over the point of the needle.

4   Pull a loop through to form the first stitch. Remove your left thumb from the yarn. Pull the loose end to secure the stitch. Repeat from * until the required number of stitches has been cast on.

THE BASIC STITCHES

The knit and purl stitches form the basis of all knitted fabrics. The knit stitch is the easiest to learn. Once you have mastered this, you can move on to the purl stitch.

Knit stitch

1 Hold the needle with the cast-on stitches in your left hand, with the loose yarn at the back of the work. Insert the right-hand needle from left to right through the front of the first stitch on the left-hand needle.

2 Wrap the yarn from left to right over the point of the right-hand needle.

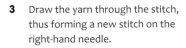

3 Draw the yarn through the stitch, thus forming a new stitch on the right-hand needle.

4 Slip the original stitch off the left-hand needle, keeping the new stitch on the right-hand needle. To knit a row, repeat steps 1 to 4 until all the stitches have been transferred from the left-hand needle to the right-hand needle.

Purl stitch

1 Hold the needle with the stitches in your left hand, with the loose yarn at the front of the work. Insert the right-hand needle from right to left into the front of the first stitch on the left-hand needle.

2 Wrap the yarn from right to left, up and over the point of the right-hand needle.

3 Draw the yarn through the stitch, thus forming a new stitch on the right-hand needle.

4 Slip the original stitch off the left-hand needle, keeping the new stitch on the right-hand needle. To purl a row, repeat steps 1–4 until all the stitches have been transferred from the left-hand needle to the right-hand needle.

INCREASING AND DECREASING

Many projects will require some shaping. This is achieved by increasing or decreasing the number of stitches you are working.

Increasing

The simplest method of increasing one stitch is to work into the front and back of the same stitch. On a knit row, knit into the front of the stitch to be increased into; then, before slipping it off the needle, place the right-hand needle behind the left-hand one and knit again into the back of it (inc). Slip the original stitch off the left-hand needle.

On a purl row, purl into the front of the stitch to be increased into; then, before slipping it off the needle, purl again into the back of it. Slip the original stitch off the left-hand needle.

Decreasing

The simplest method of decreasing one stitch is to work two stitches together.

On a knit row, insert the right-hand needle from left to right through two stitches instead of one, then knit them together as one stitch. This is called knit two together (k2tog). On a purl row, insert the right-hand needle from right to left through two stitches instead of one, then purl them together as one stitch. This is called purl two together (p2tog).

CASTING OFF

This is the most commonly used method of securing stitches once you have finished a piece of knitting. The cast-off edge should have the same 'give' or elasticity as the fabric, and you should cast off in the stitch used for the main fabric unless the pattern directs otherwise.

Knitwise

Knit two stitches. * Using the point of the left-hand needle, lift the first stitch on the right-hand needle over the second, then drop it off the needle. Knit the next stitch and repeat from * until all stitches have been worked off the left-hand needle and only one stitch remains on the right-hand needle. Cut the yarn, leaving enough to sew in the end, thread the end through the stitch, then slip it off the needle. Draw the yarn up firmly to fasten off.

Purlwise

Purl two stitches. * Using the point of the left-hand needle, lift the first stitch on the right-hand needle over the second and drop it off the needle. Purl the next stitch and repeat from * until all the stitches have been worked off the left-hand needle and only one stitch remains on the right-hand needle. Secure the last stitch as described in casting off knitwise.

SEWING BASICS

FINISHING TECHNIQUES

You may have finished knitting but there is one crucial step still to come, the sewing up of the seams. It is tempting to start this as soon as you cast off the last stitch but a word of caution: make sure that you have good light and plenty of time to complete the task.

MATTRESS STITCH (SIDE EDGES)

This stitch makes an almost invisible seam on the knit side of stocking stitch. Thread a tapestry needle with yarn and position the pieces side by side, right sides facing.

1 Working from the bottom of the seam to the top, come up from back to front at the base of the seam, to the left of the first stitch in from the edge on the left-hand side, and leave a 10cm tail of yarn. Take the needle across to the right-hand piece, to the right of the first stitch, pass the needle under the first two of the horizontal bars that divide the columns of stitches above the cast-on.

2 Take the needle across to the left-hand piece, insert the needle down where it last emerged on the left-hand edge, pass the needle under two of the horizontal bars that divide the columns of stitches. Take the needle across to the right-hand piece, insert the needle down through the fabric where it last emerged on the right-hand edge, pass the needle under the first two of the horizontal bars that divide the columns of stitches above the cast-on. Repeat step 2 until the seam has been closed.

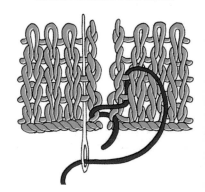

MATTRESS STITCH (TOP AND BOTTOM EDGES)

Thread a tapestry needle with yarn and position the pieces top and bottom, right sides facing outermost. Working left to right, come up from back to front through the centre of first stitch on the right edge of the seam and leave a 10cm tail of yarn. Take the needle across to the top piece, pass the needle under the two loops of the stitch above, then go down again, through the fabric, where the needle emerged on the lower piece. Repeat with the next stitch to the left.

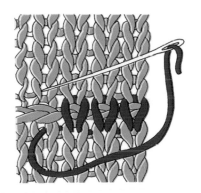

SATIN STITCH

Work a series of short straight stitches, parallel to each other, to create a pad of stitches.

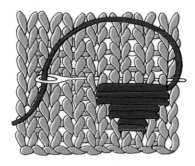

INSERTING STUFFING

As with all soft toys, how you stuff your doll will directly affect the finished appearance. It is important to stuff firmly, but without stretching the knitting out of place. Always stuff down the extremities, such as the legs and arms, first and mould into shape as you go along. The amount of stuffing needed for each doll depends on the knitting tension and individual taste.

CONVERSIONS

Needle sizes

This table gives you the equivalent sizes across all three systems of sizing needles.

Metric	US	old UK/Canadian
25	50	–
19	35	–
15	19	–
10	15	000
9	13	00
8	11	0
7.5	11	1
7	10½	2
6.5	10½	3
6	10	4
5.5	9	5
5	8	6
4.5	7	7
4	6	8
3.75	5	9
3.5	4	–
3.25	3	10
3	2/3	11
2.75	2	12
2.25	1	13
2	0	14
1.75	00	–
1.5	000	–

Weights and lengths

grams = ounces x 28.35
ounces = grams x 0.0352
centimetres = inches x 2.54
inches = centimetres x 0.3937
metres = yards x 1.0936
yards = metres x 0.9144

ABBREVIATIONS

approx	approximately
alt	alternate
beg	beginning
cm	centimetre
dec	decrease
in	inch(es)
inc	increase
k	knit
k2tog	knit two together
LH	left hand
mm	millimetre(s)
MC	Main colour
oz	ounce(s)
p	purl
p2tog	purl two together
psso	pass slipped stitch over
RH	right hand
RS	right side
sl	slip
ssk	slip slip knit
st st	stocking stitch
st(s)	stitch(es)
tbl	through back loop
tog	together
WS	wrong side
yfwd	yarn forward

AUTHOR'S ACKNOWLEDGEMENTS

I hope you all have as much fun knitting all these wonderful festive characters as I have had creating them! When I started knitting them for the Knit and Purl greeting cards I never imagined that it would lead to one pattern book let alone this, my second.

Without the inspiration, patience and support of everyone at Mint Publishing these characters would not have been created and I therefore wish to say a big thank you to all. Thanks also go to my family,

especially Alan, for putting up with my many attempts at knitting some of these characters and his gentle persuasion to keep trying.

Last but not least a big thank you to everyone at Anova Books, especially Amy and Katie. Who would have thought that when my Grandma sat down and taught me to knit all those years ago with love (and a lot of patience) that it would lead to this!

Debbie Harrold

Join our crafting community at LoveCrafts – we look forward to meeting you!